"You understand logic, don't you?"

or

the early days of Digital Computing in the British Army

By Ken Anderson MSc

"You understand logic, don't you?"
or
the early days of Digital Computing
in the British Army

Written and compiled by Ken Anderson MSc

Published by Las Atalayas Publishing

First Edition 2005
Second Edition 2007

ISBN 978-0-9556-753-6-2

Design and Typesetting by kenandglen.com

Ken Anderson joined the Army as an apprentice radar mechanic in April 1958. He spent the majority of his adult military career serving with the Royal Artillery. Much of that time was spent seconded to civilian companies, developing and manufacturing military equipments. During those secondments, he was involved with the development of *FADAC, EVA* and the automatic test equipments for the *Rapier* missile system. He was also closely involved with the introduction into service of the *Green Archer* mortar-locating radar and served with 3RHA on active service with its deployment to Borneo, during the Indonesian confrontation in the mid 1960s.

On completing his military service, Ken was employed at the *Plessey* research laboratories at Roke Manor, as a member of the system trials unit during the development of *Ptarmigan*, the secure digital battlefield communications system.

Later employed as an electronic system consultant with *EASAMS (Elliott Automation Space and Military Systems)* he was a key member of the project management team for the design and development of the electronic and computerised dynamic positioning system on the Royal Navy's Seabed Operations Vessel (SOV).

In the late 1980s, Ken established his own digital computer systems company, providing system design and services to the Admiralty Underwater Weapons Establishment at Portland and to a number of defence manufacturing companies.

In 1995 he became a self-employed technical consultant to the *Group 4* conglomerate of security companies advising them on a range of technological matters to create some custom business software solutions to their problems.

In 2001, after returning to college, he was awarded a Master of Science (MSc) degree in Multimedia Technology and continues today with his interests and activities in electronics and computing although now retired to the sunny climes of Spain.

"You understand logic, don't you?"

or the early days of Digital Computing in the British Army

Introduction

At the start of the third millennium, personal computers, laptops, notebooks, personal organisers, and an enormously wide range of digital computers, are now commonplace, with even very young children being aware of what they are and how to use them. In fact, many people today - and particularly younger members of the Armed Forces - have never known a world without them. But, as recently as the early 1960s, digital computers were mostly unheard of and there were certainly none in use by the British Army.

There were, and had been for nearly two decades, a range of equipments using analogue computers, although they were perhaps not recognised as such. Examples of such were the No.11 Predictor, used with the heavy anti-aircraft system for the 3.7" HAA gun, the 3Mk7 Fire Control (FC) radar and the 4Mk7 Tactical Control (TC) radar. The 7Mk4 *Yellow Fever* light air defence radar had a very sophisticated electromechanical analogue computer and the 8Mk1 *'Green Archer'* mortar-locating radar had a very neat and compact integral analogue computer. Older readers would no doubt be able to identify several more such examples.

This article, as well as recounting my own early experiences in this field, attempts to place into some historical context how the first digital computer was introduced into service with the British Army.

1

Larkhill

Having completed a three-year Army Apprenticeship at Arborfield, I passed out from the Apprentices' School in December 1960, as a Class 3 Radar Technician. My early months of 1961 were spent attending a 2nd Class upgrade course at No.5 Training Battalion REME, also at Arborfield. In the late spring/early summer of 1961, I was most fortunate to be sent to the Trials Unit (TU) of the School of Artillery, Larkhill, my first working posting as a shiny and wet-behind-the-ears L/Cpl Class 2 Radar Mechanic!

Although I was on the establishment of the TU, I was actually working in the Radar Section of the School of Artillery, Workshop REME. At that time, the only equipments were the 3Mk7 FC and 4Mk7 TC radars. My first task was to work with some MoD scientists, on experiments regarding the luminance and persistence of Plan Position Indicators (PPIs) & cathode ray tubes (CRTs) in the 4Mk7s. That summer was most enjoyable as, when not working, several of us were busy building and flying model aircraft. The weekends were long and the excellent bus services enabled everyone to go home to wherever they seemed to live in the UK. These were still the latter days of National Service and there was tremendous camaraderie between the regulars and NS guys, celebrated weekly with cheese and biscuit evenings in the billets and a once-monthly night out in Amesbury, to enjoy good ale and beef sandwiches at one of the local hostelries.

Out of uniform and into civvies

Towards the end of the summer, I was called into the Tiffy's office, to be told that I was to attend a two-week course with some civilian firm in North London, to learn about a piece of equipment that the School of Artillery Trials Unit was shortly to receive. I reported first to the Royal Engineers (RE) Postal Depot in Mill Hill, where I was to be billeted. Then, donning civilian dress, I reported to the firm of *Elliott Bros (London)*, in Elstree Way at Borehamwood, just a ten- or fifteen-minute bus ride away. I had no idea of what I was going to do and arrived with just a duffle bag, containing a SO 421 notebook and a few pencils. After being introduced to who I now know was one of the senior company managers, I was taken down to the factory floor and introduced to the chief engineer, who was standing alongside rows of gleaming electronic equipment cabinets. These were *Elliott 803B* digital computers, in various stages of construction and commissioning.

2

Fig 1 - A typical Elliott 803B Computer Suite

His first words to me were, *"You understand logic, don't you?"* To which I immediately replied, *"Yes"*, as in ordinary language, 'logic' (from the ancient Greek *logice*=sense/think) is the reasoning used to reach a conclusion from a set of assumptions. Immediately upon my positive reply, he passed me an enormous A1-sized folder, full of what seemed to be engineering drawings or circuit diagrams; and then guided me to a small office, where he told me to get on and study the contents! Of course, these drawings turned out to be the logic diagrams of all the components and circuit boards of the *Elliott 803B* digital computer!

Within the next few days, I quickly began to understand what computer logic was all about – the use of a 'logic gate' as the elementary building block of digital circuits.

I had been told, prior to leaving Larkhill, to expect to spend two weeks at *Elliott Bros*, learning about a new piece of equipment for the Royal Artillery (RA) gunners. Within a few days of my being there, it quickly became obvious that the equipment destined for Larkhill hadn't yet even been built! As a result of this, I was to spend some three months at Borehamwood, quickly becoming a valued member of their engineering team. The team was commissioning a number of *Elliott 803Bs* for sale to some large commercial companies and banks, while I was still wondering what the application of such a computer could be for the RA.

The *Elliott 803B* was housed in three cabinets, each 1.42 metres high, and 0.4 metres deep and with a total length just over 2.5 metres. Such a size was considered to be quite compact in 1961! The first of these cabinets housed the power supply units, consuming some 3.5 kilowatts and based around an on-line battery charger and large accumulator. This design was effectively an early form of uninterruptible power supply (UPS), well able to cope with any fluctuations and interruptions in the mains power supply, from which all the logic circuits were powered. Having become accustomed to large electro-magnetic circuit breakers and contacts in the 4Mk7 radar, it was most surprising and enlightening to come across a mercury tilt-switch for the very first time.

The *803B* was the first second-generation computer, in that it used transistors, as opposed to thermionic valves, and ferrite core memory. The components were mounted on a very basic design of printed circuit board (PCB), where most of the detailed signal wiring was 'discrete', in that single-core lengths of wire were used to interconnect the various elements. Each of these PCBs had four multi-pin in-line connectors, enabling then to be easily plugged in or out of the computer backplane for maintenance. The majority of transistors used on the logic boards were early germanium junction type, such as OC42s and OC45s. These were encased in small

Fig 2 - The 803B Core Store cabinet and voltage monitoring panel

glass phials, which were painted black. One problem frequently encountered was that the black paint would get scratched and, if a door to the cabinet containing the circuit board was opened, some light could fall onto a transistor on one of the circuit boards, causing it

Fig 3 - Early germanium transistors

to switch from one logic state to another - thus making faulting finding quite difficult at times! The later metal-case encapsulated transistors, such as the OC72, obviously didn't suffer from the same problems. All of these PCBs, together with the main memory store, were housed in the second and third cabinets, together with the main core memory store.

Computer memory

The *803B* had just 4K words of core memory (equivalent to about 20Kbytes) that, by today's standards, seems extremely small. Each core memory consisted of a stack of memory planes, with each memory plane having tiny magnetic cores with a fine mesh of interlacing wires crossing through them. Each core could be magnetised one way or the other, thus signalling a '0' or a '1' in the binary numbering system needed by the digital computer. On each memory plane, there were 1024 of these tiny magnetised cores, each representing just 'one bit' of information. Thus, each of these ferrite cores held a single bit of binary information, whereas today millions of bits of information rest in a tiny single integrated circuit.

The amazing interlace of wires and tiny magnetic rings are long gone now, but their legacy still lives on in the words 'stack' and 'core memory'.

Each core held a single bit, while the

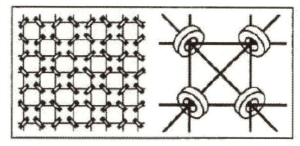

Fig 4 - Schematic of Ferrite Ring storage

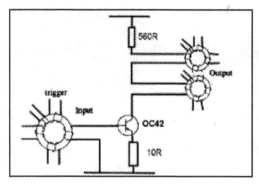

Fig 5 - A typical 803B logic element

magnetic polarity of the core held the bit value. To write a bit, there were 'X' and a 'Y' wires. To read a bit, there was a sense wire. The read process consisted of writing a value to a specific core, indexed via the X and Y wires. If the core 'flipped' magnetic polarity, the sense wire would 'see' it, and the computer would know the bit had been of opposite polarity. If the sense wire did *not* detect a flip, then the bit value was the same as the one being currently written. Either way, the bit had to be rewritten.

These memory plane stacks were constructed by women, using stereo microscopes, who worked hour after hour stringing, by hand, the wires through these cores, standing up on edge with their holes all perfectly lined up. The wires, thinner than a human hair, had long 12- to 24- inch stainless 'needles' attached to the end, simply for rigidity. The wire, although very thin, was insulated with *'Formvar'*, a high resistance material that could be stripped with heat. The women would tediously string these rows and rows of core with the needle/wire assemblies, cutting the end of the wires close to the appropriate solder land to complete the core planes or stacks.

The CPU

Unlike today's modern computers and PCs, where the Central Processor Unit (CPU) is a single chip, some 90% of the PCBs in the *803B* held the various circuits to make up the CPU. These comprised a number of registers - known as the Accumulator or 'A' Register; a Sequence Control Register or 'SCR'; a 'B' Register and an Auxiliary Register. Together with master oscillators and arithmetic circuits, such as a 'half adder', the registers provided all the functional components for a bit-serial machine. As data was handled serially, it was most important to ensure that merging data streams arrived at a logic gate at the right moment in time, to within a fraction of a microsecond. To achieve this, some circuits incorporated acoustic delay lines, to provide the necessary delay. These took the form of a helix nickel wire, with pulses of current representing bits of data passed through a coil surrounding one end of the wire. These were converted

Fig 6 - Stack of Core Stor planes

into pulses of mechanical stress, due to the 'magnetostrictive' effect. A receiving coil at the other end of the helix was then used to convert the pressure waves back into electrical pulses. These devices were originally developed at *Elliott's* Borehamwood laboratories, another 'first' for British inventiveness.

Input / Output

As with today's modern computers, the *803B* needed some ancillary devices to handle the inputting and outputting of data. It also required a control console to switch the computer on and off, to initiate and control the operation of the auxiliary devices and to allow the operator to execute simple sequential command and operations. The Control Console is pictured in Fig.4 although its correct name was 'The Word Generator".

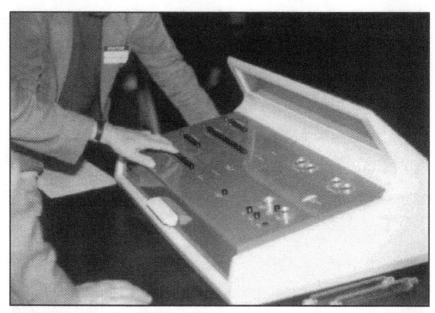

Fig 7 - The Word Generator or Control Panel

The large buttons at the top right were for switching on and off the main power and the computer battery or logic power.

The group of push buttons below had control functions, whilst the four rows of buttons to the left were used to program the computer. The 803B used a 39-bit word length. This was divided into two 19-bit instructions, with a so-called 'B-bit' completing the 39. Within each of those instructions, the first 3 bits were used to specify the instruction group, the second 3 bits the instruction type and the remaining 13 bits to specify an address or input/output function.

The two sets of 3-bits were defined as 'Octal', whilst the 13-bit part was 'binary'. Thus, with the buttons set as follows 101 010 0001100010001 (where a '1' indicated the button depressed), this would be interpreted as: Execute instruction 52 (five two, not fifty-two) on store location 785 - or in plain English multiply the contents of the accumulator by the contents of store location 785. Although this seemed quite mind-blowing on first encountering the console, one quickly became adept at converting decimal numbers into both octal and binary quantities. (As an aside, I was to be faced with a similar task some ten years later, when working with the designers of the *'Rapier'* missile automatic test equipment, as that system used 16-bit hexadecimal word strings).

8

On the front face of the console was a horizontal bar, what could perhaps be called the 'space bar' on a modern 'qwerty' keyboard. This was pressed each time an instruction entered on the push buttons was to be entered. There was also a loudspeaker on the console; this was driven from a logic element monitoring the number of 'jump' executions performed by the computer, thus producing a variety of different sounds. After some time spent using the computer, these sounds became quite recognisable and various operations performed could be readily recognised. It was also possible to write small programs, producing musical tunes - a good party-piece when demonstrating the computer to visitors, who had never even seen a computer!

Although the Word Generator could be used to input sequential commands one-by-one, this was a most tedious process. In 1961, there were certainly no floppy disks, CDs, DVDs or magnetic disks of any sort. Magnetic tape was available for audio applications, but its use for the storage of computer data was still being developed, with much of that work being undertaken at *Elliott's* Borehamwood laboratories. Their initial work was based upon magnetic tape sub-systems, using modified film handlers - of the kind used in movie studios, instead of the more familiar half-inch tape

decks. The principles were that the same oxide coated celluloid tape passes near a multi-channel read/write head, but that the 'tape' was conventional 35mm film stock coated with oxide, whilst the mechanism included sprockets and spring-loaded tension arms. A clue to the origin of this technological cul-de-sac may lie in the address of *Elliott's* computing division in Elstree Way, Borehamwood - Elstree in the 1950s and 60s was the heart of the British Film industry. The films were

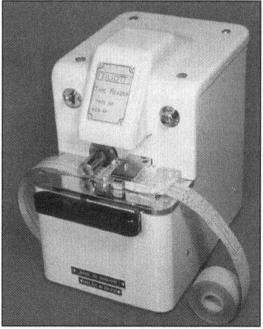

Fig 8 - Elliott Optical High Speed Tape Reader

Fig 9 - The Paper Tape Station

specially made by *Kodak* and formatted at their factory, although the *Elliott* service engineers could effectively reformat them, by using a special film copy program to replicate a known good tape.

In 1961, the major means of inputting and outputting data from the computer was by punched paper tape. Paper tape had been around for some time and was commonly found in teleprinters, telegraph and telex machines. However, they were relatively slow devices, outputting their tape only as quickly as the keyboard operator could type. *Elliott* designed and manufactured their own optical high-speed paper tape reader (PTR), capable of reading 5-hole paper tape at 500 characters per second. It was fascinating to watch a large reel of paper being read and then spewed out of the reader! A Teletype high-speed tape punch was an electro-mechanical device capable of punching tape at 100 characters per second and this was the primary means of outputting data, either for storage or to present the results of computations. Paper tape was a most unreliable medium, as it was subject to tearing, becoming dirty or affected by humidity. (Once I was back at Larkhill, I conducted trials with a variety of different paper and plasticized tapes to try and determine the most suitable for use in a hostile military environment).

Computer circuitry

As mentioned earlier, the logic circuits consisted of a germanium transistor and a ferrite core, typically as shown in Fig.5. As the ferrite cores were very small and extremely delicate, they would be encapsulated in a small plastic block, typically the size of a series-74 integrated circuit. There were about six or seven different types,

Fig 10 - Teletype High Speed Paper Tape Punches

some having just a single ferrite core and some with two and a variety of windings. Fig.10 shows a typical 803B circuit board where the logic elements can be clearly seen – the encapsulated ferrite cores are the small rectangular shaped bricks - and the resistors and transistors can be clearly seen. As so can the discrete hard wiring of the trigger pulses, from pins on the top of each ferrite core unit. The development of germanium transistors (especially those to be used in a switching mode as opposed to

Fig 11 - A typical 803B circuit board showing the discrete components

11

linear amplification modes) and encapsulated ferrite cores in those early years was really stretching the boundaries of electronic development. There was a tremendous spread of characteristics in the manufacture of semi-conductors that impacted tremendously on their reliability.

Once an *803B* had been assembled, commissioned and fully tested on the assembly, there was still a most important phase of testing to be conducted, even though the computer may have been run for many hours and days (soak testing was still a technique in its infancy). The final stages of testing involved moving the complete system – CPUs, Control Console and Paper Tape Stations - into an environmental chamber, known as the 'hot and cold' room. Here, the complete computer system would be tested over a period of four or five days, while the temperature was gradually raised from its ambient operating of 20° C to some higher level and then lowered below that ambient. This resulted in the failure of perhaps some 1 - 2% of some individual components. Once this final testing was completed, the *803B* was determined 'fit', to be shipped to the customer.

Goodbye to Borehamwood

By this time I had spent nearly three month at Borehamwood; first as a visitor with no knowledge of digital computers; but then as an integral member of the engineering commissioning team. I now had a good knowledge of the construction and design of the *803B*, computer logic and the digital design techniques of the time. However, I still had no idea as to the application that the Gunners at Larkhill had for a digital computer. This was about to be rapidly put right! The *803B* destined for the Army was packed up and prepared for shipment – not to the School of Artillery, but to *Elliott Automation* at Rochester Airport, in the Medway Towns in Kent! So I said goodbye to my billet at Mill Hill and made my way to a new one in a RE barracks in Chatham, located on a hill just above the dockyard there. This was a good location for, as I was quickly to find out, there were plentiful pubs on its doorstep and a NAAFI Club just half a mile away! The barracks were a couple of bus trips away from Rochester Airport, for a journey that took about half an hour. On first arriving at Elliott Automation, I was introduced to a small design team, who I was to work with for the next six months. Yes, that original two-week course eventually turned into a nine-month civilian deployment.

It was then that I learnt the reason for the Army buying the *803B* digital computer and exactly what the project was to be.

Fig 12 - The Elliott 803B Central Processor and Core Store cabinet

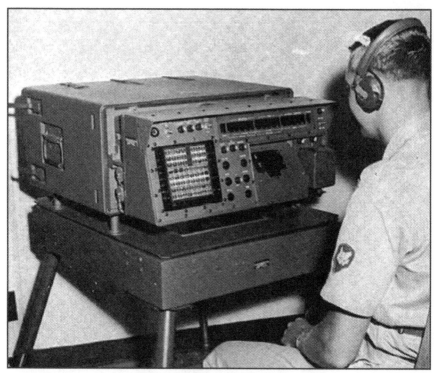

Fig 13 - The US Army Fadac

Fig 14 - The US Army Fadac in the field

The Royal Artillery mission

Before continuing it is probably worthwhile to discuss the place or function of the RA (field artillery) in the British Army.

The mission of the field artillery is to destroy, neutralise, or suppress the enemy by cannon, mortar, and howitzer fire and to help integrate all fire support assets into combined arms operations. Field artillery weapons are normally employed in masked or defilade positions to conceal them from the enemy. Placing the f ring battery in defilade precludes direct fire on most targets. Consequently, indirect fire must be used when field artillery weapons fire on targets that are not visible from the weapons. The gunnery problem is an indirect fire problem. Solving the problem requires weapon and ammunition settings that, when applied to the weapon and ammunition, will cause the projectile to achieve the desired effects on the target.

i. The gunnery problem may be summarised as follows:

ii. Know the location of the firing gun or battery, and determine the location of the target.

iii. Determine map data (deflection, range from the weapons to the target, and altitude of The target).

iv. Determine the vertical interval of the target and line of sight elevation.

v. Compensate for non-standard conditions that would affect firing data such as meteorological conditions.

vi. Convert chart data to firing data (shell, charge, fuse, fuse setting, deflection, and quadrant elevation).

vii. Apply the firing data to the weapon and ammunition.

The solution to the problem provides weapon and ammunition settings that will cause the projectile to function on or at a predetermined height above the target. This is necessary so the desired effects will be achieved.

In the USA, a conference was held at the Frankford Arsenal in November 1965, to present a solution to the task of solving gunnery problems with greater accuracy and speed than the conventional methods then in use i.e. of plotting tables, ballistic nomograms and slide rules. The solution presented to conference was the result of a two-year study into the basic ballistic problem, that of solving the differential equations of motion of a projectile. As a result of this conference, a set of design criteria for a calculating machine was submitted to American industry. Consequently in mid 1958, a contract was placed with *Autonetics*, a division of *North American Aviation Inc*, for the design, development and manufacture of the

Fig 15 - The UK Fadac design laboratory at Elliott Automation in Rochester

Field Artillery Digital Automatic Computer (FADAC). The first prototype US FADAC was then scheduled for delivery to and acceptance tests by the Frankford Arsenal, in late 1959 and early 1960.

Being aware of this development, the British Army approached the US Military to try and obtain a US *FADAC* on loan, for evaluation by the RA, but was unsuccessful in doing so. As a result of this, they then approached *Elliotts* to discuss the problem with them – the *Elliott* solution was to produce a facsimile of *FADAC*, consisting of an equipment physically similar, but with its computing power provided by their *803B* digital computer.

Becoming a designer

The key members of the design team at Rochester Airport were the project leader, who was a hardware design engineer and ex-Royal Navy; a software design engineer (the term programmer had still not been coined in 1961); some mechanical designers; an electronics technician and several software support staff, as well as some wireman and women. We had a nice airy office facing the airfield and a development lab in the centre of the building.

Adjacent to our laboratory were several other offices and laboratories, with tightly guarded access - as *Elliott Automation* at that time was heavily involved in the *TSR2* fighter aircraft project. It was obvious that I was most welcome there, as I quickly became involved in both some electronic design work as well as some software program engineering. The first task for all of the team was to construct the *FADAC* look-alike or simulator. The computer produced for the US Army can be seen in Figs.13 & 14. Photographs of the one designed and produced at Elliott Automation can be seen, then in the early stages of development in our laboratory, in Figs.15 & 16 (a photograph of the completed FADAC is shown on the front cover). This was to represent as closely as possible the US machine in shape, look and functionality - but with all its computing power provided by the *Elliott 803B*.

The simulator was constructed to hold a number of circuit boards similar to those used in the *Elliott 803B* itself. However, instead of using the germanium transistor, ferrite cores and other discrete elements of the *803B*, it used some brand new devices called *Minilogs* (mini logic elements). These were plastic encapsulated elements, of a small rectangular block format, approximately 50mm long, 20mm wide and 15mm high, with ten or twelve pins for fixing into the PCB. These were the latest developments from *Elliott's* Borehamwood laboratories and were, in some respects, the forerunner of the integrated circuits to be first seen in the latter half of

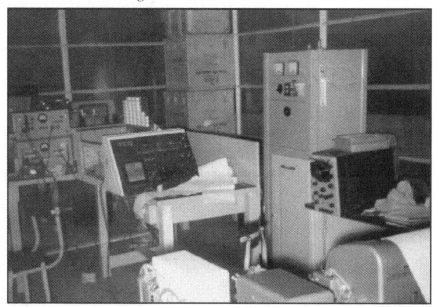

Fig 16 - A photograph of the the UK FADAC during its design and development

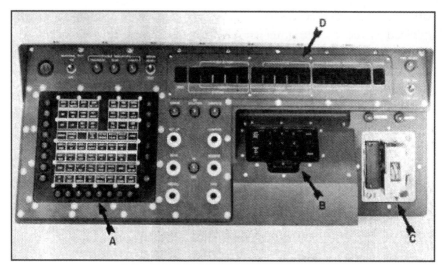

Fig 17 - The US Army FADAC front panel

that decade. These PCBs contained the necessary electronics to interface to the host computer that would then be connected by one or two multi-core cables each 50 metres in length. They also contained some local processing capability, as well as the interfaces to the input and output devices of our *FADAC*.

The significant features of the input output devices on the front panel layout can be seen in Fig.17, which shows the US *FADAC*. The Matrix Input group (A) consists of a matrix of sixty-four indicators, each of which was selected by depressing one of eight buttons in the vertical row and one of the eight in the horizontal row. Each of these sixty-four represented a specific input function, such as the grid location of the gun (northings, eastings and height) or that of the target. Once a function had been selected, its numeric value was punched in, using the manual keyboard (B). The keyboard was of an electromechanical design that gave a very satisfying 'clunk' feeling in its operation - if my memory serves me correctly! Once the computation had been completed, the solution was displayed on a numerical display (D) of 15 *Nixie* tubes. These were electronic devices for displaying numerals, in the form of glass tubes containing multiple cathodes and a wire mesh anode. They were filled with neon gas and often a little mercury and/or argon, at a small fraction of atmospheric pressure. Although resembling a thermionic valve in appearance, their operation did not depend on the heating of a cathode to cause it to emit electrons and were often called cold cathode tubes. The

Nixie tubes had eleven cathodes, in the shapes of the numerals 0 to 9, with a decimal point. Each cathode could be made to glow in the characteristic neon red-orange colour, by applying about 170 volts DC between it and the anode. Whilst the US *FADAC* had a mechanical tape reader (C), which was used for the inputting of meteorological data, on its front panel - this was not necessary in ours, as we had the benefit of the optical high speed tape reader with the *803B* itself. These three primary input/output devices employed quite different power supply voltages and currents – thus it was not only necessary to interface them correctly, but also to provide the necessary power supply units.

The power supplies were outsourced from a UK manufacturer and perhaps were the only item that provided us with any form of reliability problems. Strange however that, throughout the next forty years of my career in electronic engineering, computers and information technology problems with power supplies seemed to raise their heads again and again!

Understanding the specification

Whilst the hardware design was continuing apace, the senior software engineer was making tremendous progress with the design of the computer programs on the *Elliott 803B* digital computer.

These programs provided solutions to the field artillery support computations of surveying and reduction of meteorological data from radio sondes as well that of the differential equations of projectile motion from firing to impact. All the programs were written in 'machine code', as programming languages were only just starting to be produced at that time. There was something called *Elliott Autocode*, designed by *Elliott's* Tony Hoare, who later went on with his wife and a J S Hilmore to develop the *Algol* programming language. We did however have the benefit of a library of sub-routines that were most useful, considering that we only had 4K of memory to use for both the programs and the data.

Early in 1962, both the hardware and software were sufficiently developed to be able to demonstrate the system to a team from the MoD and from the School of Artillery. The first problem and solution to be demonstrated was where the target was at 90° east of the gun battery. The necessary co-ordinates and gun data were punched in and the 'compute' button hit. Immediately, the solution was displayed on the *Nixie* tube display, in the form of a bearing and elevation for the gun in mils – an answer of 1571!

The *FADAC* design team stood back with big smiles of their faces saying, *"Isn't that great?"* whilst the gunners stood there in abject dismay. No one from the military side had told the design team that, in military gunnery, there were 6,400 mils in a circle and not '1000 x 2π' or 6,283 milli-radians! This was a lesson well learned, not only for *Elliott* but also for myself, one which I never forgot as my career developed, for I was to work with many more civilian companies on development projects, both while still serving in the Army and later as a civilian.

Fit for service

The *803B* was a commercial digital computer, designed for use in an environment that was strictly controlled in terms of temperature and humidity. At that time, custom-built computer rooms were just starting to be constructed in the major banks and commercial companies. These would normally have suspended floors, allowing interconnecting cables and other services to be run underneath them and hidden from view. They would also be fully air conditioned and environmentally controlled. Our 803B was to be installed into two 3-ton trailers (see Fig.15) and towed around the Larkhill artillery ranges - something the designers at *Elliott* had never contemplated!

A special cradle, constructed from angle iron and rectangular section steel tube, was mounted on anti-vibration mounts and shock-absorber feet, in one of the 3-ton trailers. With some of the cosmetic panels removed,

Fig 17 - The 3-ton trailers housing the Elliott 80B computer

the three cabinets of the *803B* were then mounted and secured within this cradle. Before proceeding any further with the installation of the computer into the trailer, a number of accelerometers were fitted in various locations on and in the computer cabinets and connected to some recording devices. The trailer was then towed around the Kent roads and highways for a day, to measure the shock and vibration experienced by doing so – but no cross-country testing at that time! The Paper Tape Station and the table for the Word Generator were then mounted, again on anti-vibration mounts, in the second trailer. Although the trailers were fitted with air conditioning units, it was necessary to install night storage heaters in each of them, to ensure that overnight the computer was kept at a comfortable 60° F.

The trailers had obviously originally been used for some electronics or telecoms application (although I was never able to discover their history), as each one had a cable access panel on the left-hand side. These were removed and replaced with new panels, on which were mounted a number of *Plessey* Mk4 connectors. The cabling and wiring between the computer and paper tape station and control panel was split and terminated at these connectors with a number of multi-core cables, each one metre in length and also using *Plessey* Mk4 connectors used to connect the two trailers together.

Back into uniform

During the nine months, spent first at Borehamwood and then at the Medway Towns, I had enjoyed a life much different to that of the previous four years, as an Army Apprentice and a uniformed soldier. I had enjoyed the benefits of lunching in the Managers' Restaurant each day at Borehamwood, with regular visits to London's West End in the evenings. At Rochester Airport, I had made good friends with the rest of the *FADAC* design team and enjoyed a very good social life with them throughout my time there. But the design phase of the project was now complete and it was time to move back to Larkhill. A couple of 10-ton trucks arrived one morning and hooked up the two trailers, now completed fitted out, to tow them back to the School of Artillery. On our arrival there, they were initially parked in the secure Guided Weapons Park, as no one was sure of the security status of the project.

This was a little disconcerting, for after nine months as a free agent, it meant being back in uniform in a disciplined environment, with lots of REME senior ranks around to keep their eyes on me. Fortunately, that situation lasted only for twenty-four hours, as a decision was made by the Trials staff to move us up to the Gun Park behind the Regimental Headquarters of the School. Then, although in uniform, I was again a free agent, reporting only to the RA trials officer, who was a Capt Peter Sexton. My only contacts with the REME Workshop were when I used to borrow a 3-ton *Commer* Radar Repair vehicle (RRV) when out on the ranges!

For the next six months, life consisted of deploying *FADAC* on a series of trials on the Larkhill ranges, with live firing 25-pdr guns, 5.5" guns, 105mm pack howitzers and the FV433 *Abbott* 105mm self-propelled gun. Both *FADAC* and the *Elliott 803B* proved to be most reliable, thus the amount of time spent on repairs and maintenance were minimal.

This gave me plenty of opportunity to increase my computer programming skills, which was to prove so beneficial later in my career. The gunners took advantage of this, as I produced a number of programs for them - one to take the raw data from the Electronic Velocity Analyser (EVA), used to calibrate the muzzle velocity of guns, and another to do with the deployment of nuclear warheads.

Fig 18 - The FACE Prototype Model A developed in the mid 1960s's
With WO2 AQMS Keith Evans at the keyboard

22

Conclusion

At the end of the trials period, and having spent some fifteen months of my life learning a great deal about digital electronic computers, the project was brought to a successful completion. The use of such a computer as *FADAC* was rightly deemed as the way forward for the solution of the gunnery problem.

A year later Elliott Bros were just starting to develop their 18-bit word length *900* series of digital computers, which were physically much smaller than the *803B*. A joint proposal from them and the MoD resulted in a full development contract being placed with them, for the design and development of a ruggedised computer for the RA. This, based on the Mil Spec 920, was to become the *Field Artillery Computer Equipment (FACE)*, which eventually came into service in the second half of 1969 and was to be deployed world-wide with all RA field artillery batteries until the early 1990s.

Personally, I was most pleased to have been so involved in this, the introduction of digital electronic computing into the British Army. The engineering and technical skills, knowledge and experience gained in those early years was to benefit me enormously throughout the rest of my career, both in the Army and afterwards. This was particularly so in learning and knowing how to write software programs efficiently in machine code as I was most fortunate in later years in having access to some of the first microprocessors to reach the UK and develop applications using them. That of course is another story.

Acknowledgements:

Many thanks to Bill Purvis and Tony Finn for help in refreshing my memory and for some of the photographs of the *Elliott 803B* computer.

<u>The Computer</u>

One of the most important parts of the computer is the store. This can best be compared with a set of numbered pigeon-holes each of which can be used to store information. This information can be either data or an instruction. The number of each LOCATION is referred to as its ADDRESS. Each location will hold one computer WORD i.e. an array of bits. All the computers we will be concerned with have a fixed word length i.e. number of bits in each word. The word length may vary from computer to computer i.e.

The 803 has a 39-bit word length
The 502 has a 20-bit word length
The 920 has a 18-bit word length

When the information in a store location is an instruction it will consist of at least two sections

(i)   the operation or FUNCTION to be performed

(ii) the address of the data

Functions can be divided into three main groups:

1.   Arithmetic Operations, e.g. Add, Subtract, etc.

2.   Control Operations, e.g. "Now go to location X" for your next instruction. "

3.   Data Transfers (i)   Input and Output

                     (ii) Store to register transfers

In addition to the store, several other registers are required. In a fixed word-length machine most of these have the same word-length as the store.

One of the more important registers is the ACCUMULATOR This register is used in most data transfers e.g. from one store location to another or from store to an output device. However, its primary use is in arithmetic operations, e.g. in addition, two data sources are required, one is the store location specified, the other is the accumulator. Thus the instruction ADD N means add the contents of N to the contents of the accumulator

The other important register is the SEQUENCE CONTROL REGISTER (S.C.R.) This is the register which determines the

Pages from an Elliott computer programming course manual produced in 1964.

24

next order to be obeyed.   In some early machines it was
necessary to divide each order into three sections:-

1.   Function

2.   Data source for function

3.   Address of the next order

        It is obvious that a more convenient method is to assume
sequencial operation through the store except where otherwise
specified.   Thus a program starting at location X will take its
next order from X + 1 then X + 2, etc.   This process is
achieved by adding 1 to the S.C.R. as each order is obeyed.
The process will continue until the computer meets either (i) a
STOP order or (ii) a control order i.e. JUMP TO N.   Many
computers have a stop order included in their order code.
However we will more frequently use the JUMP order to stop the
computer e.g. If we wish to stop the computer at location 2,
the order JUMP TO 2 will do this.   It is convenient for the
computer operators to be given some signal when an order is
being obeyed continuously - on the 803 this is an audible signal.
The above sequence controlling instruction is called an
unconditional jump.   Frequently computers have instructions
which will only cause a sequence interrupt when an arithmetic
register is in a specified state, e.g. JUMP IF ACCUMULATOR
IS NEGATIVE.   This is called a conditional jump.

Other Registers

        Some arithmetic operations (e.g. Multiplications) double
the number of significant digits i.e. 5 x 5 =   25
                                      .5 x .5 =   .25
                                      500 x 500 =   250000

        It is therefore convenient to be able to temporarily retain
these double length numbers.   This is achieved by the use of an
extension to the Accumulator called the AUXILIARY REGISTER.
This register is normally intended only for double length
operations.   Therefore, operations such as Add, Subtract, etc.
can usually not be performed on the Auxiliary Register.

        There is frequently another register accessible to programs,
known as the Modifier Register (or more commonly the B-REGISTER
since it is secondary to the A-Register or Accumulator).   A

detailed description of this register will be included in the study
of individual computers.   At this stage it should be sufficient
to say that the instruction which is taken from the store is
modified by the contents of the modifier register before it is
actually obeyed.   The modification is called upon when required
by the presence of a specified bit as a group of bits in the
location holding the instructions.

There are many other registers within each computer
which are not accessible to programs - nevertheless the
registers influence the operation of the computer and in some
computers it is necessary to know more about these additional
registers

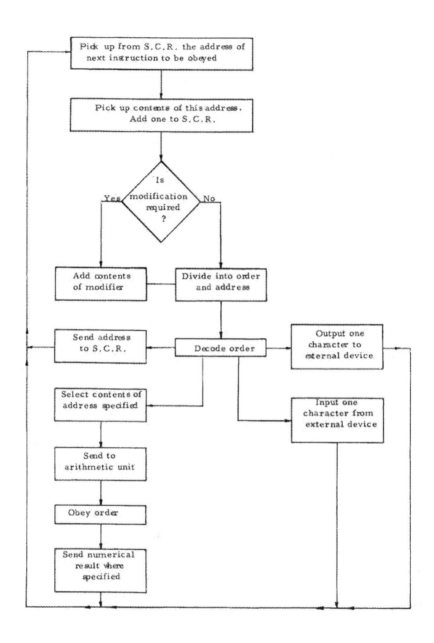

Flow Chart

A Brief History of the Royal Regiment of Artillery

There have been gunners ever since the invention of guns in the 13th century, and the first official gunners were appointed in 1485, as part of what became the Board of Ordnance. Throughout the next 400 years the forts around Britain had master gunners permanently appointed by the Board of Ordnance. Trains of artillery were formed for campaigning both at home and abroad, with guns and the men to serve them.

1716 to 1800

In 1716, under a Royal Warrant, two companies of artillery, each of 100 men, were formed at the Woolwich Warren (later the Royal Arsenal) to ensure that a regular force of gunners was available when needed. Woolwich has been the spiritual home of the 'Gunners' ever since that time, although the Regiment had moved to its famous barracks on Woolwich Common by 1805. The Regiment expanded rapidly in the 18th century and saw service in every campaign and every garrison world-wide. In 1793, the Royal Horse Artillery was formed to provide greater mobility in the field, and soon became associated with the role of supporting cavalry. The RHA performed so well that it became a corps d'elite within the Regiment. The 19th century The 19th century saw the Regiment heavily engaged in the Crimean War and the South African War. Throughout the century, it was campaigning in India alongside the separate artilleries of the East India Company. This led to their amalgamation with the British Army after the Indian Mutiny, bringing some famous batteries into the Regiment. The 20th century

The science of artillery grew rapidly under the pressure of the Industrial Revolution and by the end of the 19th century, the need for indirect fire brought major changes. Guns became ever more powerful, firing more efficient munitions to longer ranges with increased accuracy and greater speed. The Great War of 1914-18 was to prove an artillery war, and the number of gunners increased dramatically, serving 6,655 guns by the end of the war, with anti-aircraft (AA) guns joining in against the new threat from the air. The inter-war years provided active service on the fringes of the Empire, but the 1930s saw the Regiment once again arming for war. Full mechanisation now replaced the horses which had served the Regiment for so long. In the war which ensued, the Regiment again provided firepower in every theatre, on land, at sea in the Maritime Artillery, and in the air with Air Observation Posts. Gunners manned huge numbers of AA guns both in the field and in the home base. Many of the AA Regiments were formed from Territorial Army units. Most of the Light AA gunners began the war as infantrymen.

Despite the reduction of the Army in the post-war years, the Regiment has been armed with some of the most potent, long-ranged weapons it has ever manned. Today it uses the wide span of technology of all the Arms, with virtually no branch of military science unexplored.

But the Regiment's history is the foundation stone on which it rests. For over 280 years of unbroken service since 1716, and reaching back a further 400 years to the first bombard, artillerymen have provided the Army with the firepower it has needed in Defence and attack. In 1833, King William IV recognised that to continue granting Battle Honours to the Regiment would result in an excessive list, and granted instead a single Battle Honour, the motto Ubique (Everywhere), with an accompanying motto Quo Fas Et Gloria Ducunt (Whither Right and Glory Lead).

Today, the Royal Regiment of Artillery forms a powerful and complex branch of the Army. It is the only section of the Army which has employed Nuclear weapons, and during the Cold War formed one of the premier deterrents to a Soviet Armoured advance through Central Europe. US and British Lance missiles would have almost certainly been used to even the odds, the far-outnumbered NATO Armoured forces would have had to face.

Indirect fire forms the Artillery's second role, providing a depth of fire designed to disrupt, delay and destroy enemy forces before they can come into contact with friendly forces. And in the third role, defends the mobile Army from air attack. Although it did have the role of Anti-tank Swingfire operation for a time, that role has been absorbed by the Royal Armoured Corps.

The Royal Regiment of Artillery has operated in its existence everything from light cannon, to huge siege pieces, through to the end of the Cold War and Nuclear Weapons, and now onto the realm of smart munitions and the MLRS. Today the Royal Regiment of Artillery is combined with the Royal Horse Artillery to form the Royal Artillery.

Events from the History of the Royal Regiment of Artillery

1346 - Battle of Crécy. First recorded use of cannon.

1544 - Term "Train of Artillery" noted for the first time.

1678 - Appointment of Master Gunner of Whitehall and St James's park instituted.

1716 - First two Companies of Artillery formed br Royal Warrent at Woolwich.

1720 - Title 'Royal Artillery' first used.

1722 - Royal Regiment of Artillery of four Companies formed.

1741 - Royal Military Academy formed in Royal Arsenal at Woolwich.

1748 - Presidential Artilleries of Bengal, Madras and Bombay formed.

1756 - Royal Irish Regiment of Artillery formed.

1762 - RA Band formed in Minden (oldest British orchestra).

1782 - RA moved to current RA Barracks (Front Parade) on Woolwich Common.

1793 - First Troop of Royal Horse Artillery Formed.

1801 - Royal Irish Regiment of Artillery incorporated into the Royal Artillery.

1805 - Royal Military Academy moved to Woolwich Common for RA and RE Officers.

1819 - Rotunda given by Prince Regent to celebrate end of the Napoleonic Wars. - First military museum and training centre.

1832 - Regimental Mottoes granted.

1855 - Control of the Royal Artillery was transferred from the Board of Ordnance to the War Department.

1859 - School of Gunnery established at Shoeburyness, Essex.

1862 - Presidential Artilleries of Bengal, Madras and Bombay transferred to the Royal Artillery.

1920 - Rank of Bombardier instituted in the Royal Artillery.

1924 - The Royal Regiment once more became one Regiment.

1947 - The Riding Troop RHA was renamed The King's Troop

1951 - The appointment of Colonel-in-Chief became Captain General.

The Royal Regiment of Artillery

When guns were needed to serve at home or abroad, a train of artillery had to be authorized by a royal warrant, and it was disbanded again on the cessation of hostilities. This system led to much confusion and delay, and in the Jacobite Rebellion of 1715 it took so long to mobilize a train that the rebellion was over before the guns were ready.

It was then decided to organize a permanent force of artillery, and so on the 26th May 1716 two companies of artillery were created by royal warrant of King George I and were formed a Woolwich. Six years later on 1st April 1722 these two companies were grouped together with companies at Gibraltar and Minorca to form the Royal Regiment of Artillery, Colonel Albert Bogard being appointed as its first Colonel.

During the eighteenth century the Regiment continued to grow and by 1757 there were 24 companies apart from the Cadet Company formed in 1741. They were divided into two battalions of 12 companies each, with appropriate staffs. In 1771 there were four battalions consisting of eight companies and an additional two Invalid companies each, the latter being raised for garrison duties in order to free other companies for active service overseas.

Civilian wagons and horses were still being hired to move the guns and it was only in 1794 that the 'Corps of Captains Commissaries and Drivers' was formed to provide drivers and teams for the field guns. (The RHA formed in 1793 already had its own horses and teams for each troop). In 1801 this Corps was replaced by a similar organisation called the Corps of Gunner Drivers. This was also unsatisfactory, and in 1806 its title was changed to the Royal Artillery Drivers. Finally in 1822 this Corps (already greatly reduced in establishment since 1815) was disbanded and recruits were enlisted as 'Gunner and Driver'. This continued until after 1918 when enlistments were made as Gunner only.

In 1833 King William IV granted the Regiment the privilege of bearing the Royal Arms over a gun with the Motto UBIQUE (Everywhere), followed by QUO FAS ET GLORIA DUCUNT (Whither right and glory lead). In 1855 the Board of Ordnance was abolished, and the Royal Artillery, together with the Royal Engineers, came under the Commander-in-Chief and the War Office like the rest of the Army.

In 1859 the companies ceased to be organised into battalions, and were brigaded instead, at the same time being referred to as batteries instead of companies. In 1861 after the Indian Mutiny the Royal Artillery received the addition of 21 troops of Horse Artillery and 48 batteries from the three Indian Presidencies, and so now comprised 29 RHA batteries, 73 field batteries, and 88 garrison batteries.

On 1st July 1899 the Royal Artillery was divided into two distinct branches – mounted and dismounted. A royal warrant established the Royal Garrison Artillery as a separate Corps from Royal Horse Artillery and Royal Field Artillery, and decided that it was to man the Coast Defence Units, the Mountain Batteries, and the Heavy and Siege batteries. However, this decision was reversed in 1924 and both branches were united into a single Corps – The Royal Artillery.

In 1938 the decision was taken to mechanise the Horse and Field Artillery, and to adopt a new organisation for these units, and for the medium artillery. In place of 'brigade' the term 'regiment' was substituted.

On 1st April 1947 all batteries except RHA were placed on a single roll. Batteries were numbered on this roll throughout the whole regiment, so that there was only one battery bearing any particular number.

Changes after the second World War comprised the abolition of Anti-Tank Artillery, and in the middle of the 1950s the abolition of the Anti-Aircraft Command and the entire Coast Artillery organisation.

In 1993 after the Strategic Defence Review the Royal Artillery was cut down to 17 Full Time Regiments (Inc 4 RHA) and 7 Territorial Regiment.

The Royal Horse Artillery

Until the end of the 18th century gunners had to walk beside their guns, which meant that movement was slow. On many occasions the officers (who were mounted) had to manhandle the guns into action before their men arrived.

The solution was obvious and in January 1793 two troops of Horse Artillery were raised, differing from field units in that all personnel were mounted. Two more troops were formed in November 1793, and each troop had six 6-pounder guns with 45 drivers and 186 horses on their establishment, a self-contained mobile fighting unit of artillery had at last come into existence. The superior organisation of the RHA troops enabled them to develop from the first a very high standard of discipline and efficiency, which has never been allowed to weaken.

After Waterloo, seven troops of RHA were disbanded between 1816 and 1819 (including 2nd Rocket Troop) and the others were reduced to a skeleton establishment, barely sufficient to man two guns apiece. Nevertheless the corps survived, and after the Crimean War the Royal Horse Artillery was formed into a Horse Brigade. In 1861 the Horse Artillery batteries from the Indian establishment increased the strength by four brigades, making a total of five. In 1871, under the stimulus of the Franco-Prussian War, a further reorganisation took place, whereby one RHA battery was added to the Regiment, making a total of 31 batteries in the RHA. Six years later, however the RHA was again reorganised, this time into three brigades (10 batteries and one Depot Battery to each brigade). In 1882 the brigades were reduced to two (each of 13 batteries) and a depot (a reduction of 5 batteries). Following the outbreak of the South African War in 1900 there was an increase of 7 batteries, and during the 1st World War the Regiment expanded to 50 RHA batteries. But the end of the war brought the inevitable reductions, and by 1936 the strength was 3 brigades and five unbrigaded batteries, a total of 14 batteries. By 1940 the batteries were mechanised, except for a ceremonial RHA Troop in London (The Riding Troop).

In 1947 King George VI inspected the Riding Troop (which had been formed for ceremonial duties) at St. John's Wood. He created history by erasing the title of the troop and inserting the words 'The King's Troop' a title which Queen Elizabeth II was pleased to leave unchanged.

In 1959 there were five RHA Regiments with a total of 15 batteries and the King's Troop making the sixteenth. But by 1969 further reductions had taken place and the strength now comprises:

The King's Troop RHA
1st Regiment RHA
3rd Regiment RHA
7th Parachute Regiment RHA

"REME exists to keep the punch in the Army's fist"
(Field Marshal The Viscount Montgomery of Alamein)

Maintaining and Repairing the Army's equipment has always played an important part in ensuring the fighting efficiency of the Service. Until the late 19th century, however, the relative simplicity of the equipment in use with the Army made a specialist corps of tradesman unnecessary. The soldier carried out minor repairs on his own equipment, assisted as necessary by the armourer, the regimental farrier, the carpenter and the leatherworker.

The First World War provided a major impetus to the production of technologically advanced military equipment. The machine gun dominated the battlefield until the introduction of the tank. The wireless set and the motor vehicle made their first appearance in the arena of war and, overhead, the machines of the Royal Flying Corps demonstrated that technology would henceforward play a vital part in the conduct of military operations

At first, the maintenance and repair of this new equipment was carried out ad hoc by the users but, as the quality of machinery increased, the need for a rational system was clear. In the post First World War years, therefore, the responsibility for the repair of tanks and some of the motor vehicles was added to the armament repair function of the Ordnance Corps.

In 1926 this became the Royal Army Ordnance Corps (RAOC). The three other corps which used specialised equipment on a large scale (The Royal Engineers (RE), Royal Signals (R SIGNALS) and Royal Army Service Corps (RASC)), were generally responsible for the repair and maintenance of their own equipment, and had their own engineers and workshops.

The early years of the Second World War brought the realisation that the existing repair system was not able to support the massive scale of equipment being deployed in every theatre. In 1941 the War Cabinet directed Sir William Beveridge to carry out an enquiry into the employment of technical manpower in the Services. As a result of the recommendations of this enquiry, the Royal Corp of Electrical and Mechanical Engineers was formed on 1st October 1942.

The First Members of the new Corps were engineers and tradesmen from RAOC, RE and RASC, supplemented by the transfer of skilled man from other units. By May 1945, REME had proved to be indispensable and had expanded in response to the scale, variety and deployment of the weapons and equipment in service until it numbered 8,000 officers, 150,000 soldiers and 100,000 civilians. From its inception, REME was deemed to be a combat corps, and REME detachments served in the front line in every major theatre of operations.

After the Second World War, demobilisation and the need to return technical manpower to industry bought about the last major adjustment to the organisation of the Corps. In 1951, REME assumed responsibility as the technical agency for almost all of the Army's equipments and engineering manpower which remained on other units was units was transferred to REME. Since then the functions of the Corps have increased in line with technological progress, and the REME soldier has provided engineering support for every military operation of significance.

Operational Tours have included roulement tours (rolling system of tours) in Northern Ireland since the trouble began in 1969, the Falklands war in 1983, the First Gulf War in 1991, Angola, Zaire, Iraq (Op Safe Haven), Bosnia Herzegovina, Afghanistan and in 2003 the Second Iraq War. These roles have presented many challenges to REME in what have often been harsh and unforgiving engineering environments. The roots of REME may therefore be considered to be in the engineering branches of four of the major corps on the Army and it is this evolutionary lineage, and the distinction of having been forged in the furnace of war, which forms the foundation of the tradition of the Corps.

Full historical details of REME can be found in these two books - Craftsmen of the Army Volume I (1942 to 1968) and Craftsmen of the Army Volume II (1969 to 1992) both of which are avilable from the REME Museum of Technology at Arborfield.

Museums

Firepower - Royal Artillery Museum

Royal Arsenal, Woolwich, South East London

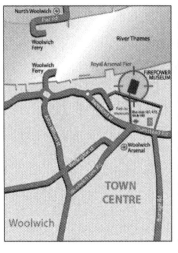

The Royal Artillery Museum has been open to the public since 4 May 1820, a record we believe to be unrivalled by any other military museum.

In May 2001 the collection of Artillery was moved to the new premises within the gates of the Royal Arsenal and opened under the re-badged name of "FIREPOWER, The Museum of the Royal Artillery." The museum had returned to the original home of the Regiment and indeed of the collection. The collection was founded in 1778 at the Royal Arsenal by Captain (later Lieutenant General Sir) William Congreve.

Firepower, the Royal Artillery Museum in Woolwich tells the powerful and dramatic story of artillery, scientific discoveries made through warfare and human stories of courage and endeavour. The 'ground shaking' Field of Fire audio-visual show puts you in the midst of battle as shells whiz overhead and guns roar. drawings, diaries and medals bring together some 700 years of world artillery history.

REME Museum of Technology

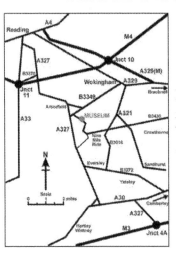

Arborfield, near Reading, Berkshire.

The Museum has an interesting display of REME through the years and collections including Weapons, Electronics, Historic Vehicles, Aeronautical Engineering, Medals and Corps Archives.

The Museum is normally open daily excluding Saturdays. It is closed at Christmas, New Year and Easter. There is a Café for light lunches and snacks.

Computer Museum - Bletchley Park

National Museum of Computing in Block H at Bletchley Park.

Built in 1944, Block H was designed to house the world's first digital computers, the Colossus machines. The museum will allow visitors to follow the development of computing from the ultra secret pioneering efforts of Colossus, the post war innovations of the 1950s, through the mainframes of the 1960s and 1970s, and the rise of personal computing in the 1980s. Using original systems restored to working order with the help of the BCS's Computer Conservation Society, the museum will encourage visitors to operate and learn from our exhibits, and enjoy using machines they once used, programmed, or simply played with

The Museum started with the acquisition of an Elliott 803 mainframe and this machine is on long term loan. The machine was in a sorry state and has been gradually restored to working order by John Sinclair, the longest standing current curator.

The 803 is now surrounded by computers from around the globe both from the early years of analogue through to the latest technology of Pentium chips and 3D graphics. With the exception of the 803 and some of the old calculators, the exhibition is very much hands-on and visitors are encouraged to reminisce on machines of their past or try their hand at something different.

The Museum is staffed entirely by volunteer curators. The majority of them are in full time employment and give up weekends to maintain and develop the exhibits and to provide information and assistance to the visitors.

Index

Symbols

105mm pack howitzer 22
25-pdr guns 22
35mm film 9
3Mk7 1
4Mk7 1, 4
5.5″ gun 22
7Mk4 1
8Mk1 1

A

'A' Register 6
Accumulator 6
Algol 19
Amesbury 2
Army Apprenticeship 2
Autocode, Elliott 19
Autonetics 15

B

'B' Register 6
ballistic nomograms 15
Borehamwood 2, 9

C

Central Processor Unit 6
connectors, Plessey Mk4 21
core memory 5

E

Electronic Velocity Analyser 22
Elliott 803B 2, 22
Elliott Automation 12
Elliott Bros 2
Evans, Keith 22

F

FACE 23
FADAC 16, 22
ferrite core 11
Field Artillery Computer Equipment 23
Finn, Tony 23
Frankford Arsenal 15
FV433 Abbott 22

G

Green Archer 1
Guided Weapons Park 21
H
Hilmore, J S 19
Hoare, Tony 19

I

integrated circuit 11

K

Kodak 10

L

Larkhill 2, 10, 20

M

Medway Towns 12
milli-radians 20
Mill Hill 2
Minilogs 17

N

National Service 2
Nixie tubes 18
North American Aviation Inc 15

O

OC42 4
OC45 4
OC72 5
Octal 8

P

Paper tape 10
paper tape reader 10
Paper Tape Station 21
Paper Tape Stations 12
Plan Position Indicators 2
plotting tables 15
power supply units 19
Predictor, No.11 1
printed circuit board 4
Purvis, Bill 23

R

Radar Repair vehicle 22
Rapier 8
REME 21
Rochester Airport 12
Royal Artillery 15
Royal Engineers 2

S

School of Artillery 2, 19
Sequence Control Register 6
Sexton, Capt Peter 22
soak testing 12

T

transistor, germanium 11
TSR2 17

W

Word Generator 7, 9, 21

Y

Yellow Fever 1

www.ingramcontent.com/pod-product-compliance
Lightning Source LLC
Chambersburg PA
CBHW051217050326
40689CB00008B/1340